How to Build the

Shellback Dinghy

How to Build the

Shellback Dinghy

by Eric Dow

Photographs by Sherry Streeter

Published by:
    WoodenBoat Publications, Inc.
    P.O. Box 78, Naskeag Road
    Brooklin, Maine 04616-0078

Library of Congress Cataloging-in-Publication Data

    Dow, Eric, 1954–
        How to build the Shellback dinghy/by Eric Dow; photographs by Sherry Streeter.
        p.   cm.
        ISBN 0-937822-27-2: $15.00
        1. Dinghies—Amateurs' manuals. 2. Boatbuilding—Amateurs' manuals.
        I. Title.
        VM351.D68   1993
        623.8'2026—dc20

Introduction

There's a bit of irony behind the publication of *How to Build the Shellback Dinghy*. In 1984, we asked Joel White, Brooklin's resident naval architect and boatbuilder, to design for us a simple, seaworthy, beautiful plywood tender, the result of which was the Nutshell Pram in two versions. So highly successful was the Nutshell Pram in concept and construction that we simply put aside any thoughts of developing the ideas further. Fortunately, however, Joel White could not resist experimenting further himself, and he proceeded to design a skiff-bowed boat, built exactly the same way, and a bit longer overall, for those who might need or want such a boat. It was a solid, if quiet, success, and several boats were built to the design by employees of Brooklin Boat Yard, and then regularly raced in Center Harbor.

Although I should have known better, I was not at first as enamored of the design as I later became, and I rowed and sailed only the one which had been built of lighter, cheaper stock than the usual high-grade mahogany plywood. This combination of factors resulted in my failing to look further into the attributes of the design, and we never arranged to sell the plans for the Shellback through WoodenBoat. Instead, Joel himself sold them directly to interested customers. In the meantime, I asked Joel if he would design a somewhat longer, stiffer boat, more suited to our average user, and the result was the Pooduck Skiff, a fine and reliable—if somewhat less thoroughbred and lively— boat. It too, was a success.

During the summer of 1992, Joel asked if I'd be willing to tow his Shellback behind our cruising boat FREE SPIRIT to Newport for the WOOD Regatta being held in conjunction with The WoodenBoat Show. We usually tow our peapod, but she's a little too heavy to bring aboard if the weather turns really bad offshore in the Gulf of Maine, and I knew we could bring the Shellback aboard if we had to. There is hardly a better, more quiet and docile boat to tow than a peapod, so we departed Brooklin with high standards and moderate expectations. It was quite a surprise, then, to find the Shellback exceeding those expectations from the moment we stood out to sea.

To begin with, she rode the seas like a duck, floating lightly as could be, and yet firmly in the water. Under ordinary conditions, she towed straight and true, ranging forward only in stronger following seas, and even then, tracking well. If the following seas grew larger, she could tow a bight of line to provide a little drag, and once again she stayed where she belonged. At our first anchorage following the passage, we were taken with how beautifully she rowed—quick and responsive, and yet tracking well. Sculling—with a single oar over the transom—was equally easy. Picking up a small family ashore, we found her as able as ever, fully loaded. And under sail, she was quick and nimble, and yet quite secure for an open boat in moderate breezes. Thus it was that I began to realize how severely I had underestimated her capabilities when I had first looked over the boat.

When the Show was over, we towed her home without incident, and I placed an order with a local builder, Eric Dow, for one of our own. I also spent several repentant moments with Joel White apologizing for failing to look more closely at the prototype, and for relying on a somewhat more quick-and-dirty version in my judgments.

The following summer we set off for Newport again with our own Shellback in tow, this time with 35 knots of northwest wind on our quarter. That wind held for several hours out into the Gulf of Maine, later diminishing to about 20 knots, and by the next morning, to just a few knots as we neared the Cape Cod Canal. Although we'd been watching the trim of the Shellback regularly for evidence of seawater throughout the day and night, we finally brought her alongside for a close inspection once inside the Canal. To our surprise and delight there was no more than a half cup of water in her, a testament to her ability to ride high and dry in a seaway. Two days later, she finished first among several Shellbacks in the Newport WOOD Regatta (winds reported 20–30 knots) under the skillful hand of Maynard Bray. (Note: Any open boat can quickly fill and swamp, especially in gusty winds, and although the Shellback *itself* will float when swamped, flotation added under the seats will provide even more positive buoyancy.)

As a modern, all-around small boat, or an easily cared-for tender, the Shellback seems pretty hard to improve upon. A skilled builder can construct the sailing version in about 100 hours from scratch, and a kit version is available which goes together in considerably less time. As a teaching tool, the Shellback provides an education in the fine points of sailing, rowing, and sculling for sailors of all ages, her standing lug rig easily dropped altogether if the winds come on too strong. She is not easily adapted to outboard power, primarily because the weight of the motor throws her fine hull out of trim, but she rows well enough to provide plenty of efficiency and speed, even with a load. Finally, she can be decorated with as much or as little varnish as you like, and she lends herself to a variety of paint schemes. She is distinctive enough in appearance to attract admiration at every turn, a unique blend of traditional design and modern wood construction. If you have chosen to embark on the construction of a Shellback, you will find the entire experience thoroughly gratifying.

The step-by-step construction sequences covered in the following pages were written by Eric Dow, who not only builds and repairs boats here in Brooklin, but also teaches boatbuilding here and in the Pacific Northwest. Eric has built a number of prototypes for us, and it is he who prepares the stock for Nutshell and Shellback kits. Because he has thought a great deal about how these boats go together, it is very gratifying to provide another forum for his expertise.

The construction photographs were taken by Sherry Streeter, who made herself available during the many crucial stages in order that we could produce as clear a manual as possible. A former art director of *WoodenBoat* magazine and designer of many of WoodenBoat's books, she brings an eye for both detail and design to her photography. She is also my wife and sailing partner, and thus brought a special interest to the construction of this Shellback for us.

Joel White, the designer of the Shellback as well as many other boats small and large, wrote the section on rigging and sailing. It is always a special privilege to include his thoughts in any project we embark upon, and his experience in getting the most out of the Shellback under sail is particularly valuable here. He is a demon sailor in just about anything, but his ability to sneak through a fleet of Shellbacks in a race is downright uncanny.

The Shellback dinghy is a wonderfully versatile little boat for sailors of all ages, and a wonderfully practical boat for these times. She is precisely the kind of boat we like to offer; the experience of building, rowing, sculling, and sailing her encourages an appreciation and an understanding of design, construction, and traditional seamanship. Moreover, it is an experience and understanding readily shared with family and friends. Our fondest hope is that we will see fleets of Shellbacks everywhere.

The instructions herein are designed to guide both the builder of the kit and the builder from scratch using plans. Information regarding the purchase of plans or kits will be found on page 56.

Jon Wilson, Editor
WoodenBoat Magazine

Building the
Shellback

Kit Parts List

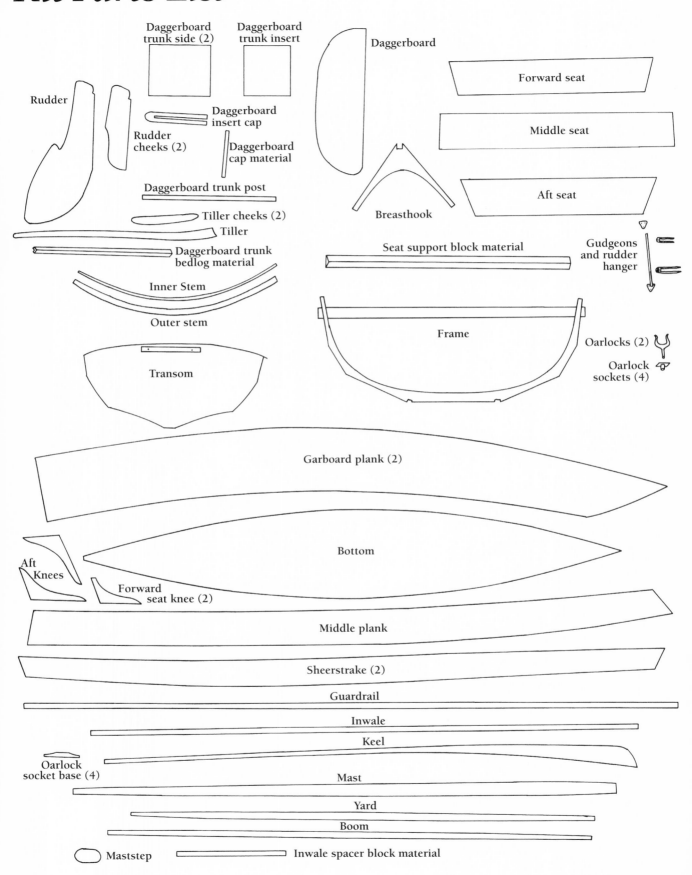

- Daggerboard trunk side (2)
- Daggerboard trunk insert
- Daggerboard
- Rudder
- Rudder cheeks (2)
- Daggerboard insert cap
- Daggerboard cap material
- Daggerboard trunk post
- Tiller cheeks (2)
- Tiller
- Daggerboard trunk bedlog material
- Inner Stem
- Outer stem
- Transom
- Forward seat
- Middle seat
- Aft seat
- Breasthook
- Seat support block material
- Gudgeons and rudder hanger
- Frame
- Oarlocks (2)
- Oarlock sockets (4)
- Garboard plank (2)
- Bottom
- Aft Knees
- Forward seat knee (2)
- Middle plank
- Sheerstrake (2)
- Guardrail
- Inwale
- Keel
- Oarlock socket base (4)
- Mast
- Yard
- Boom
- Maststep
- Inwale spacer block material

2

Materials List

Bottom from one sheet (4 × 10') of $\frac{1}{2}$" (12mm) mahogany plywood (SNBCC, Bruynzeel, or equal in quality).
Rudder blade, daggerboard, and trunk sides will come out of the remainder of this sheet.

Side planks from two sheets (4 × 12') of $\frac{1}{4}$" (6.5mm) mahogany plywood (SNBCC, Bruynzeel, or equal).
Rudder and tiller cheek pieces will come from remainder.

Stem from 14 pieces $\frac{1}{8}$ × $1\frac{3}{4}$ × 42" fir or mahogany strips to laminate as shown. Finished siding to be $\frac{7}{8}$".

'Midship frame from enough $\frac{1}{8}$ × $\frac{1}{8}$" fir or mahogany strips to laminate as shown. Finished siding to be $\frac{7}{8}$".

Transom from $\frac{3}{4}$" (18mm) mahogany plywood as above. Requires piece 18 × 36".

Seats from 38"-, 40"-, and 50"-long pieces of 1 × 8" cedar or pine.

Guardrails from two pieces $\frac{5}{8}$ × $1\frac{1}{4}$" oak or mahogany, 12' long.

Inwales (optional) $\frac{1}{2}$" × $\frac{7}{8}$" × 12' from oak or mahogany .

Knees and breasthook from enough $\frac{7}{8}$ × 6" mahogany to make four knees and two breast-hook pieces.

Seat support blocks from $1\frac{1}{2}$" × $2\frac{1}{2}$" × 5' mahogany.

Keel/skeg from $\frac{7}{8}$" × 5" × 10' mahogany.

Daggerboard trunk logs from one piece $1\frac{1}{8}$ × $1\frac{3}{4}$ × 27" mahogany.

Daggerboard trunk posts from one piece $\frac{9}{16}$ × 1 × 25" mahogany.

Maststep from one piece $1\frac{1}{2}$ × $3\frac{1}{2}$ × 6" oak or mahogany.

Tiller from one piece $\frac{7}{8}$ × 3 × 42" mahogany or oak.

Spars:
Mast from one piece 3" × 3" × 10' spruce; may be glued up from two pieces of 2 × 4' clear spruce.
Boom from one piece $1\frac{3}{4}$" × $1\frac{3}{4}$" × 10' spruce.
Yard from one piece $1\frac{3}{4}$" × $1\frac{1}{2}$" × 9' spruce.

Oars: One pair $7\frac{1}{2}$' spruce or ash oars.

Oarlocks and sockets.

Rudder hangers: One set suitable hardware, available from: The WoodenBoat Store or The Anchorage.

Painter from at least 15' of $\frac{3}{8}$" Dacron rope.

Halyard, sheet, and traveler from about 55' of $\frac{1}{4}$" Dacron rope.

Two $\frac{3}{4}$" round brass thimbles or small blocks, three small bronze or stainless eye straps, one #1 bronze snaphook.

Belaying pin: 5" long, from oak, locust, or bronze.

Epoxy glue.

Paint and sandpaper.

Chafing strip: $\frac{1}{2}$" half-oval brass; about $12\frac{1}{2}$' needed.

Fastenings: all bronze
 Wood screws:
   $\frac{3}{4}$" #8 FHWS plank to guardrails;
   1" #8 FHWS plank to transom, stem, and frame;
   1" and $1\frac{1}{4}$" #10 FHWS bottom to keel;
   2" #12 FHWS seats to support blocks;
   $\frac{3}{4}$" #6 FHWS chafing strip to keel and stem;
   $1\frac{1}{2}$" #10 FHWS transom to knees;
   assorted screws as needed.

Machine screws:

One $\frac{1}{4} \times 4''$ bottom to keel;

six #10 × 1″ rudder hanger to transom;

sixteen #10 × 1$\frac{1}{4}$″ oarlock sockets to guardrail;

two $\frac{1}{4} \times 2\frac{1}{2}''$ maststep to bottom.

Tools

Claw hammer

Block plane

Smoothing plane

Spokeshave

Butt chisel, about $\frac{3}{4}''$

Crosscut handsaw, fairly fine

Hacksaw

Tape or folding rule

Framing square

Combination square

Sliding bevel square

Spirit level

Set of twist drills in sizes to $\frac{1}{4}''$

Countersink

Small electric drill with $\frac{1}{4}''$ or $\frac{3}{8}''$ chuck

C-clamps, about a dozen 4″ to 6″

Sharpening stone for edge tools

Manual screwdriver—the type of your choice as long as its bit fits the screw slots

Pencils

Wood rasps

Mill file (for metal)

Putty knife

Scraper

Center punch

Optional tools that will make the job go more quickly

Bandsaw

Sabersaw

Electric drill press with $\frac{1}{4}''$ or $\frac{3}{8}''$ chuck

Variable-speed electric or cordless drills for drilling holes and driving screws; two will make the job go faster

Regular and drywall bits for drill/ screw gun

Portable electric plane

Bench grinder (for sharpening edge tools)

Combination taper drills/countersinks for the screw sizes used

Cutting the Pieces and Laminating the Stem and 'Midship Frame

1 After studying the plans package to get an overall feel for the task at hand, pull out the full-sized pattern sheet and begin. The patterns allow the builder to bypass the lofting process and transfer the shapes of the station molds, 'midship frame, and transom directly to wood. Here, points are being pressed along a mold station line into ½" construction-grade plywood. The drawing, secured with pushpins, has been positioned so the baseline falls along the factory edge of the plywood.

2 Once a sufficient number of points have been pressed through to determine the outline shapes of the pieces and to locate reference marks such as the centerline and sheer points, the drawing can be removed and the outline penciled in (use a batten for curved shapes).

3 Cutting as close to the line as you feel comfortable, without going into it, will make smoothing the disagreeable grain of the plywood less of a chore later. A block plane, set very fine, works well for cleaning up to the line.

4 Because I plan to build more Shellbacks in the future, I made a pattern for each piece out of thin plywood. If you're building just one boat, paper works just as well. Here, my pattern is positioned on the ¾" marine plywood transom stock and traced. This operation can also be done directly from the drawing, as were the molds.

5 The bevels for the transom edges are noted on the pattern sheet and may be sawn by setting the bandsaw table to the proper angle. This is easier to do than it appears, but if it seems too unnerving, saw the shape square and cut the bevel with a plane.

6 Shellbacks have a 'midship frame which provides strength and stiffness to the hull. It is laminated using this clamping jig. The shape, taken from the pattern drawing, has been transferred to ¾" construction-grade plywood. Here, cleats are being screwed in place to help keep the glued strips in alignment.

7 A similar jig is used for the laminated stem. This one is made of two layers of ¾" (due to the stem's greater width), fastened together.

8 The thickness of your laminations may vary depending on the type and quality of wood being used. Generally, if a single layer will bend around the shape of the jig without breaking, then a stack of many strips will also make the bend. I'm using ⅛" Douglas-fir veneer, sawn into 1¼" strips. It will take 18 strips to provide a stack of sufficient thickness for the 'midship frame. A rather thick, slow-curing epoxy is spread generously on the top surface of each strip.

9 The stack is then positioned on the jig and held there by the first C-clamp, which is installed rather loosely to a cleat. All surfaces of the jig have been lined with plastic packaging tape to ensure release once the epoxy has cured.

10 After the frame's center portion has been clamped in both directions, the ends can be sprung into place. A larger clamp here makes easier work of what can be a rather difficult push. The ends tend to slip sideways and head rapidly for your chin unless a clamp is installed to that lower cleat as well before you release your grip.

11 As the clamps that squeeze the laminations together begin to take effect, the cleat clamps can be gradually slacked off, and finally removed. Scraping off the excess epoxy while it's still wet will make smoothing the cured frame much easier.

12 The stem strips, also ⅛" thick, are glued and clamped in the same manner as the 'midship frame. A film of plastic tape was applied between the strips of what will be the inner and outer stems so that they could be laminated together and separated after cure.

13 The rough stem has been surfaced in a thickness planer to 1⅜", but could have been worked down with a hand plane. Drywall screws were temporarily driven to keep the inner and outer stems from separating while being surfaced.

14 After the screws have been removed, a slight pry separates the two stem parts. The outer stem can be set aside, and the inner one can now be cut to shape and marked with reference lines according to the full-sized pattern.

15 Here, a line of small common nails has been positioned with their heads on the outline of the center frame. By carefully positioning the frame on these nails and thumping it with a mallet in several places, the nailheads will transfer the shape. The points can then be connected with lines and the center frame sawn to its proper shape.

16 The finished frame is again positioned on the pattern sheet and a cross spall is screwed in place at the position indicated. Sheer points and a centerline are also transferred to the frame and spall.

17 The ¼″ mahogany marine plywood that we'll use for planking must be in 12′-long panels. It's sometimes possible to buy these panels pre-scarfed for length, but often more appealing (and less expensive) results can be obtained by doing this yourself. Start with three 4 × 8 sheets. Cut one in half (so it's 4 × 4), and along the factory ends of what are now four panels, draw a line 2″ in from the edge, creating the basis of an 8-to-1-ratio scarf.

18 Practically any cutting edge tool will pare away the necessary material to create an even taper, but a power plane used carefully is fast and clean. The planing of two sheets at a time is being done here at sawhorse height, with a board placed under the plywood edges for support.

19 Finishing with a belt sander has brought the scarfs to a sharp (nearly dangerous) feather edge. When the glue lines of the plies appear straight and even, it is a sign that the job has been completed.

20 While there are almost as many methods of applying pressure on a glued scarf joint as there are people scarfing, what follows is a very reliable, rather easy way. The base surface of this press is at sawhorse height. Epoxy is applied generously to the scarf surface. If you're using rather thin epoxy, it might be wise to apply a prime coat first to avoid too much penetration of the second application into the edge grain.

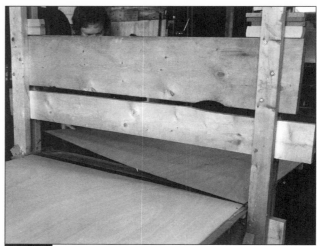

21 The adjoining panel is brought into place, aligned, and then both are screwed to the base piece to ensure they stay in position. With a plastic film both under and over this joint, a second pair of scarfed panels can be set in place and the process repeated.

22 More plastic film and a board slightly wider than the scarfed area are laid over the joint, and the sliding pressure board is lowered into place.

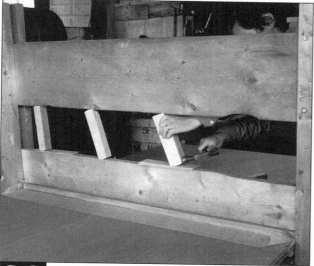

23 I used to use three hydraulic jacks for applying pressure, but have since found that wooden blocks cut to the right length and set firmly in place allow a greater feel for the amount of pressure being applied. Remember that epoxy requires less pressure than other types of glue.

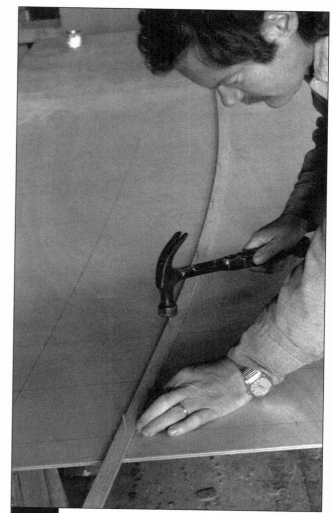

24 The Shellback layout sheet contains measurements that, when plotted at full size on a 12'-long scarfed panel, give the shapes of the hull's planks. Here, a batten is sprung and tacked along the measured points, after which it will be sighted for fairness and penciled in. Once all three planks are drawn, they can be cut out. A circular saw works well, being quick and easy to control while sawing out the long, gentle curves. Dress to the lines with your favorite plane, and proceed to use these planks as tracing patterns for their mates. Remember to transfer any reference marks (such as "frame placement") from the drawing to the planks.

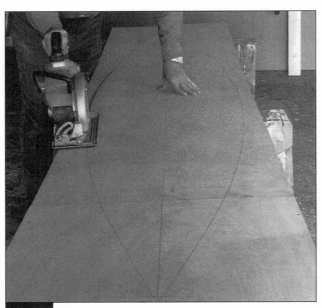

25 The bottom panel is then laid out with its centerline and mold lines as a basis for measurements. These lines are also necessary while setting up, so don't erase them. If the required 10' plywood is not available, you can scarf two pieces to length as with the sides.

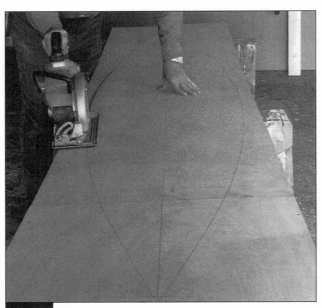

26 With the bottom cut out and dressed to the lines, you have all the pieces for the basic hull. It's now time to sweep the floor and turn attention to the setup.

Building the Ladder Frame and Setting Up

27 Setting up begins by building the ladder frame shown on the plan, using good-quality, straight, preferably dry lumber. When the ladder frame has been leveled athwartships by shimming between it and the sawhorse, it should be screwed in place. It's also helpful if the horses can be fastened to the floor.

28 The correct angle for the placement of the transom support boards is lifted from the plans with a bevel square. The boards are attached with drywall screws, as are most pieces involved in the setup. This same angle is also planed on the back edge of the aftermost 1 × 2 crosspiece.

29 Center points are marked at either end of the ladder and a chalkline is snapped between them, which marks a centerline on all crosspieces. These marks should be penciled in for future reference.

30 Here's an overview of our setup so far, along with a view of the crusty old boatshop where construction is taking place.

31 Next, the two station molds are aligned on the proper side of the crosspiece, temporarily clamped with centerlines matching, then screwed in place.

32 The 'midship frame is installed in the same way. Remember to cut the limber holes in the frame's bottom edge, as shown.

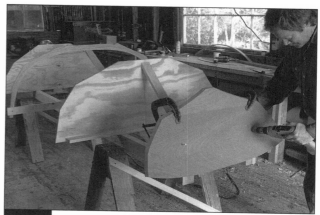

33 The temporary positioning cleat screwed to the inboard face of the transom is brought up under the ladder crosspiece and, with the centerlines in agreement, the transom is clamped to its support boards. Next, pilot holes are drilled and drywall screws driven. Onlookers may cringe at the thought of marring the mahogany transom with temporary fastenings, but these holes will be bunged later on.

34 Diagonal braces hold the molds and 'midship frame square to the ladder. Note the construction of the forward end of the building ladder, with the fore-and-aft 2 × 4 that will support the stem.

35 The forwardmost station mold is being positioned by centerlines. The plans specify the distance from the forward face of its 2"-wide cleat to the notch that will support the stem.

36 If the setup is correct, lines transferred from the full-sized patterns to the stem will fall at the top of the construction base and forward face of the forward station mold (No. ½ on the plans). If this doesn't happen, check all your measurements in this area to determine what's wrong. Before installation, plane a rough bevel on the stem's sides, using the cross-sectional view on the full-sized pattern sheet as a guide.

Planking

37 Now the exciting part begins! Dry-fit the bottom panel so pilot holes for permanent bronze screws can be drilled through into the transom, 'midship frame, and stem. A single screw is installed first at the transom so that the forward end of the panel can pivot, if necessary, into alignment. The centerline and transom mark on the bottom panel must be checked for position *before* drilling this hole.

38 A clamp is helpful to hold the forward end of the bottom panel to the stem while drilling. After you've drilled all the holes, remove the panel, clean the contact surfaces of drilling dust, apply epoxy, and reposition and screw down the bottom permanently. Temporary screws may be driven into the mold edges if the bottom tends to lift away from them.

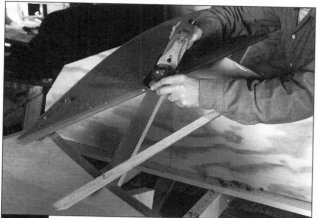

39 The edges of the bottom panel must now be beveled to give a landing for the garboard planks. Start with a very sharp plane, held at about the same angle at which molds, frame, and transom meet the bottom. Work along the entire length rather than beveling a short area at a time. Notice that a batten has been tacked in place along the surfaces about where the garboards will land.

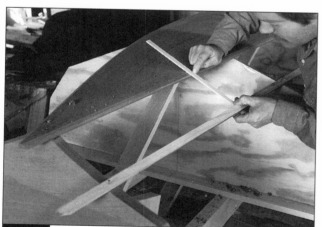

40 By holding the end of a short stick flush with the inside face of the batten, and allowing the stick to rest along the surface of the bevel, accuracy can be checked at any point between stations. Planing is complete when the bevel checks correct and the edge of the bottom has been worked down to nearly a feather edge.

41 The stem bevel should join the bottom bevel in a smooth transition; it can be checked for any needed adjustments by holding a batten across the first two molds to simulate the inside surface of the garboard where it meets the stem. The planks themselves could also be used for this purpose.

42 The garboard planks come next. Start by positioning one of them with its edge at the first knuckle of the center frame. Don't allow it to drop below this point. You transferred the "frame" marks when cutting the plank, and now with the frame placement mark determining fore-and-aft alignment, drive a small nail through the plank to hold it in place. Repeat the process at the transom. Bring the plank edge to the "second lap" mark at the stem, and tack or clamp it in place there. The plank should lie in the right place at the station molds also, but their agreement here is not as crucial as at the three permanent points. Pilot holes can now be drilled for the bronze screws that, along with epoxy, will hold the garboard planks in place.

43 Pilot holes in the transom must be drilled along a line parallel to the transom face, so the screws won't break through inside of the boat. These holes should also be set back from the plank edge so the screw won't be hit when you're planing the edge of the plank flush with the bottom.

44 It's easier to position screw holes in the rather narrow stem bevel if most of the excess plank length is marked and trimmed away first.

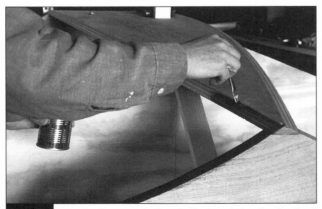

45 With all screw holes drilled and the fit checked for all mating surfaces, remove the garboards, brush away the drilling dust, and apply a generous coat of epoxy. The edges of the plywood station molds should be covered with plastic tape to prevent squeezed-out epoxy from bonding them to the hull.

46 Once the epoxy has been spread, C-clamps no longer work because the surfaces are slippery. Installing the garboard is easier if you start the first screw into the 'midship frame. This will keep the plank balanced while the ends are screwed down.

47 One method of clamping the bottom/garboard seam snugly together while the epoxy cures is to use drywall screws driven through as shown. It's not necessary to pre-drill for these. Use a variable-speed drill for driving and proceed slowly, tightening the screw just enough to pull the mating surfaces together. Over-tightening causes spin-out of the threads, and the clamping effect may be lost. Space these screws only as needed, usually every 5″ or 6″. Note: Before drywall-screwing side planks to each other, it may be necessary to support the laps from the inside in order to avoid low spots. Keep sighting for fair line. This is very important!

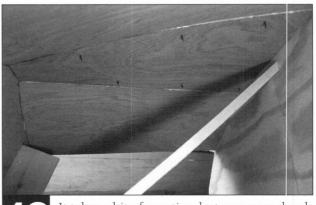

48 It takes a bit of practice, but one soon develops a feel for where to place each screw so it comes through the inside of the hull in the most effective place—close enough to the seam to produce a small amount of squeeze-out, but not so close as to split the bottom panel's edge.

49 After the epoxy has cured, remove the drywall screws and plane the garboards flush with the bottom panel as shown. This is the *only* overlap that's planed off in building the Shellback. Be sure to check that the corner you're creating at the outer face of the garboard is a nice, fair line before your neighbors check it for you.

50 With the garboards installed, the process of beveling, checking, drilling, gluing, and screwing is repeated for the mid- and sheer planks. A block plane may work better than a smoothing plane with these thinner planks, since there's much less wood to remove.

51 For the side planks near the bow, you'll need to make a transition from overlapping edges to a flush, smooth appearance at the stem. Here's one method of achieving this: The plank edge bevel is brought forward to around station ½ and checked in the usual manner. Note that a strip has been clamped to mold No. ½, extending its shape, to hold the batten in position.

52 As indicated on the full-sized plans sheet, plank overlap at the stem is ¾"; this distance is marked.

53 The overlapping plank is clamped in place using the alignment points marked on stem, molds, frame, and transom. Its opposite edge should align with the ¾" mark just made, and this edge is traced from that mark back to station No. ½.

54 The overlapping plank is then removed, and the plank edge bevel continued forward, but the bevel should not extend beyond the traced line, even if the bevel doesn't check with the batten.

55 For the planks to appear flush at the stem, we must now cut a "gain," or rabbet. This is done using a rabbet plane with a guide strip tacked along the traced line. While there is no set length for a gain, I usually start forming it about 12" aft of the stem. From this point, begin planing depth into the plank-edge bevel.

56 When completed, the gain should look something like this. At the stem face, the plank's edge is planed down almost to a feather, while ¾" away, at the traced line, we're only about halfway through the plank's thickness.

57 The overlapping plank is now clamped back in place for a second time. The fit is checked at the gain and back through station ½. Any additional bevel or gain needed will be planed into the back side of this plank. This time, before removing the plank, reach inside the boat and trace the overlapping edge of the preceding plank onto the back side of this one.

58 Now lay the overlapping plank on a work surface, inner face up. My check showed that a small amount of bevel was needed for a short distance at the forward end, but this bevel should not extend beyond the traced line.

59 Tack the guide strip along the traced line, and plane in a small amount of gain. It may take a couple of tries before the two planks fit together as they should.

60 Here's how the inner face of the overlapping plank should look after fitting. By now you've gotten quite used to putting this plank on and off the boat, so put it on one more time to drill for the screws, then it can be installed!

61 At any time during planking, the plank ends at the stern can be trimmed flush with the transom. The idea here is not to shorten the whole boat accidentally by sawing a ply or two off the transom. Work up into the cut with the saw teeth tipped slightly away from the boat, and leave a bit of plank to plane away afterwards.

62 After you've installed all the planks and while the hull is still on the building jig, it's a good time to catch up with filling and sanding. Fastening holes, plank overlaps, and any little spots that one wants to make disappear should be filled with epoxy thickened to a putty-like consistency. Faster-curing epoxy is okay here. Work it in well to completely fill the hole or seam, then scrape away as much excess as possible. Once the filler is cured, sand the hull thoroughly with a hand block or power finishing sander. A second filler application and sanding will likely be needed in some areas.

63 The plank ends are now planed flush with the inner stem. The surface created here, when complete, should measure about 1⅛" wide.

64 Remember that outer stem? It's time to find it, position it, and hold it in place temporarily with a few screws. The extra length can be left for now.

65 Mark the stem face width using a combination square and pencil. The lines for the edges of the stem face are drawn about ⅝6" either side of center.

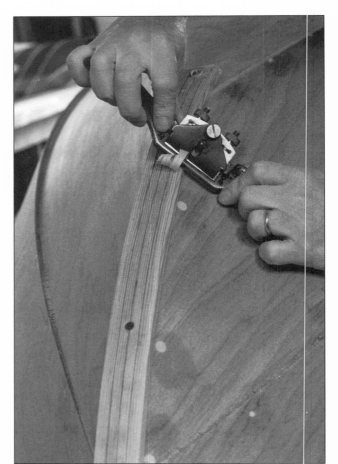

66 The sides of the stem are now beveled down to the lines you've just drawn and smoothed so they are flush with the plank surface. This can be a rather fussy job, particularly near the laps, and is best finished using a sanding block. A neat job with crisp corners makes a nice detail in the finished, painted boat. Once the bevel is complete, remove the temporary fastenings, spread thickened epoxy, and refasten with bronze screws, adding extra screws where necessary.

67 With the 'midship frame detached from its cross spall and the transom positioning cleat removed from inside (bet you forgot that), a new Shellback is born. The building jig can be put away until you build the next one.

Breasthook, Knees, and Rails

68 Now is the time, before building anything into the boat, to fill and sand the inside. The holes left by drywall screws are small and can be easily filled. Although plank laps are much less obvious than on the outside, any filling that might be necessary along the laps should maintain the nice, fair plank line.

69 My plywood breasthook patterns, lifted from the plans, are traced onto mahogany stock. Note the grain orientation, parallel with the outboard edge. The necessary edge bevels may be cut with a bandsaw at the same time you're sawing the pieces to shape.

70 The breasthook halves are tipped upward where they meet, giving a crowned effect to the finished unit and necessitating a bevel on their mating edges. Fitting here must be done carefully.

71 A fairly simple clamping jig can be made as shown. Test that it works well through a dry run, then apply epoxy to each breasthook half. Scratching these surfaces a bit first with coarse sandpaper or a rasp will result in a better gluing surface.

72 A single clamp is all that's needed to create a wedging effect that holds the halves snug while the epoxy cures. The notches in the after ends of the breasthook are to accept inwales.

73 Installation of the breasthook is accomplished by drilling and screwing through the planking, with epoxy or bedding between.

74 Although an inwale is a bit more work, it adds stiffness to the boat. Since this boat will be

fitted with one, it's necessary to notch the center frame as well as the breasthook and stern knees.

75 The stern knees are fitted to the boat so they tip up slightly from horizontal, thereby making a more pleasing line with the transom top. With the knee clamped as shown, drill the holes for screws in through the planking.

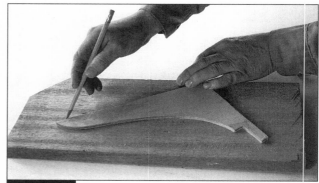

75a After making the stern knee pattern, position it as shown, then cut and fit each knee in the same manner as the breasthook.

76 There should be screw fastenings through each transom knee that are driven in from the transom. To ensure that they hit the knee correctly, the outline of the knee has been traced on the transom and pilot holes are drilled out through at the angle of the knee. After the knee has been put back, screw holes are drilled back into it and installation can be completed.

77 We turn next to the rubrails. In this photo, they have been clamped in place on the outside of the hull along the sheerline. It's important that the rails wrap around in a fair line. If, when in place, the rails don't sight in to your liking, they may be adjusted to suit and the sheerstrake trimmed to be flush. Locations for the screws that will hold the rails in place are being marked off at intervals of 5″.

78 Vertical centers are also marked using a combination square set at half the width of the rail.

79 Holes are drilled and counterbored so the screw heads will pull just below the plank surface.

80 After drilling, the rail is removed, surfaces are brushed clean, and epoxy is applied to the rail's inner face. A fairly thin coat here will prevent excessive squeeze-out.

81 Drive the first screws at the 'midship area so the rail balances, then proceed toward the bow and stern.

82 In way of the breasthook and stern knees, the screws are driven from the outside. Keep the forwardmost screw back a bit from the end of the rail to allow for some rounding.

Seats

83 Fitting the seats is easier if you make a pattern first out of thin plywood. Make the center section a couple of inches shorter than the finished product, but of correct width. The end pieces, of random length, have been cut to approximately fit the hull, after which they are clamped in place.

84 Locations of the seats, both fore-and-aft and vertical, are picked up from the construction drawings and marked on the hull. The length of the three-piece pattern is adjusted accordingly by sliding an end piece in or out.

85 The pattern ends can now be scribed to the hull, removed, and cut to fit.

86 With the pattern put back in place and fitted, the seat's end bevel is recorded with a bevel square, homemade from two ends of a broken-off hacksaw blade riveted together.

87 Drywall screws replace the spring clamps while the pattern is positioned and traced on the cedar seat stock.

88 The bevel square was used to gauge the angle of the bandsaw table so that the line and the correct underbevel can be sawn out—quickly and easily —in a single pass.

89 With the seat in place, the seat support blocks can be fitted. Trace the line of the underside of the seat onto the hull to locate the top of each block.

90 A length of stock of sufficient length for six seat blocks was milled so that the top and inboard faces were at 90°, and the surface in contact with the hull was beveled. This bevel can be adjusted slightly for each seat. The blocks are then cut to length so they set in from the seat edge ½" at either end. The inboard corners are rounded and sanded for appearance. Slight trimming may also be needed so that the block fits snugly against the "twist" of the hull. With these operations complete, the perimeter of each block is traced as shown.

91 Two pilot holes are drilled out through the hull within the block's perimeter, after which the block is repositioned, drilled (using the pilot holes) for screws from outside the hull, removed again and

brushed clean, then attached permanently with epoxy and screws. Repeat this for each of the six seat support blocks.

92 Seat fastening holes must be positioned so the screws will hit the thickest portion of the block, avoiding the sinking feeling of breaking through the planking.

93 Chamfer the bottom corners to give these 1"-thick seats a lighter appearance without affecting strength. Mark guidelines that are ⅝" down from the top and 1½" in from the edge as shown.

94 Form the chamfer with a spokeshave, plane, and sandpaper to these two lines, but stop short of the ends.

95 The chamfer fades out a couple of inches in from the ends of the seat so that full thickness occurs at the support blocks. The seats are now sanded, sealed, and set aside for the moment.

The Daggerboard and Trunk

96 The next project is the daggerboard trunk. Pick up the details from the construction drawings showing dimensions for the trunk sides and rabbeted bedlogs. Two of each are cut, aligned, and drilled for three ¾″ screws. Note that the bottom is not square to the ends. The bedlogs need not be cut to length yet.

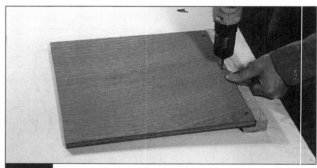

97 These mating surfaces are cleaned of dust, spread with epoxy, and screwed together. The trunk side and bedlog surfaces may be brought flush first by planing or sanding a bit if necessary.

98 The endposts are positioned flush with the edges of the trunk and drilled, epoxied, and screwed in place. Note that the posts project below the bottom of the bedlog by about an inch. These trunk sides were sawn out with a little extra height and will be cut down to their finished height later. For this reason, the upper screws are set well below the top.

99 Now place the second side against the end-posts so that the bottoms of the bedlogs are aligned with each other, and fasten it as before.

100 Once these screws are driven, assembly of the trunk is complete, and if it's not completely smeared with sticky epoxy by this time, consider yourself a neat worker.

101 Here, the assembled trunk has been trimmed and sanded smooth. The projecting ends of the posts are notched back $\frac{1}{2}''$ to form

a landing for bedding compound, and the projecting ends that remain are given a half-round shape as shown with chisel and wood rasp.

102 The trunk has to be installed to the star-board side of center, so that the dagger-board and its slot clear the outer keel. Guidelines for the slot have been marked parallel to the centerline at distances taken from the construction drawing ($\frac{9}{16}''$ + $\frac{9}{16}''$). The posts are positioned within these guidelines, with the aftermost end of the trunk against the 'mid-ship frame. The radius of each post can then be traced onto the bottom panel. These represent the ends of the slot.

103 A $\frac{9}{16}''$ hole (the width of the slot) is now bored through the bottom panel at each end of the slot.

104 Now run a sabersaw along the guidelines to remove the remaining wood to form the slot. It will probably be necessary to smooth these sawn edges with a rasp or coarse sandpaper.

105 After a bit of trimming and fussing for a tight fit, set the trunk in place with the endposts projecting through the slot. Since the bottom panel curves slightly, it will also be necessary to scribe its shape onto the bedlogs. Usually a pencil laid flat as shown will be of sufficient height for this task. Be sure the trunk is held square to the bottom panel while you're doing the scribing.

106 Trim the bottoms of the bedlogs to this scribed line. A spokeshave works well for most of the length...

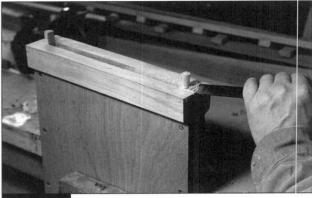

107 ...with a chisel coming in handy near the posts. Try the trunk back in place, and make any adjustments necessary for a good fit.

108 Now for the trunk top. With the 'midship seat fitted to the boat and notched around the 'midship frame and with the seat blocks in place, set the seat on its support blocks, but aft of the 'midship frame. This will allow you to set the trunk in position. Then, with a straightedge held on the seat top as shown, mark this line along the trunk side. This transfers the plane of the seat to the trunk.

109 Remove the trunk, set the seat in its proper position, and measure the distance from the bottom panel to the chamfer line (⅜" down from the seat top).

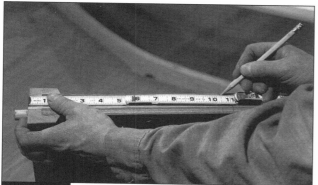

110 Plot this distance on the after edge of the trunk, starting from the bottom of the bedlogs. This is the finished height of the trunk at its after end. A new line drawn parallel to the line drawn in step No. 108 may now be drawn to intersect this height, and the trunk top cut on the bandsaw.

111 Set the trunk back in place and trace its perimeter onto the bottom panel. Plot the locations for three wood screws on each side of the slot so that they will fall roughly in the center of the bedlogs. Drill pilot holes down through the bottom at these points. Reposition the trunk and hold it firmly while screw holes are drilled back up through the bottom and into the bedlogs.

112 With the trunk removed one final time, apply adhesive bedding compound generously to mating surfaces. Then install the trunk and screw it in place.

113 The daggerboard trunk will need to be let in slightly to the center seat. Trace the trunk top outline onto the underside of the seat.

114 Chiseling this shape into the seat's chamfer will produce a notch similar to this that will greatly stiffen both the trunk and the seat itself.

The Mast Partner, Inwales, and Maststep

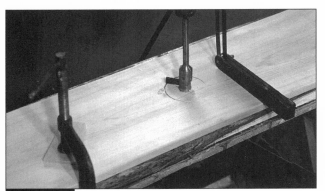

115 Now for the mast partner. An expansion bit is used to bore for the mast through the forward seat. Bore at an angle to match the bevel square you see here which was set according to the construction drawing's profile view, i.e., the intersection of the seat top and the centerline of the mast. It is now being used to sight the proper angle across to the bit.

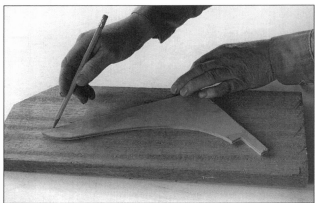

116 The knees that are fitted to the forward seat take some of the twisting strain when the boat is under sail. My plywood pattern for this knee was fitted to the boat and is now being traced to mahogany stock, with the grain running across the knee as shown.

117 With the seat temporarily screwed in place, position the knees and drill for screws through the hull. The knees will be screwed and epoxied to the hull, but not to the seat. Note that the knees set perpendicular to the hull, and that they've been notched for the inwales.

118 The inwales are spaced away from the hull, both for strength and appearance, with small blocks. These blocks are spaced as evenly as possible between the breasthook, seat knees, 'midship frame, and stern knees. They are glued and clamped in place.

119 The inwale ends are carefully fitted to the breasthook and stern knees. Here, a fine wood rasp is being used for a final adjustment. Start clamping the inwale at the breasthook end, and avoid cutting its other end for as long as possible, since the length will continue to change until the rail is completely clamped in place.

120 In this photo, epoxy has been spread on all contact surfaces, and the inwale assembly is being screwed in place with a screw through each of the spacer blocks. The screw holes were drilled during a "dry fit."

121 The time has come to smooth and detail all around the top edge of the hull. The transom top is planed to a bevel, taken from the construction plan profile view, which is closer to horizontal. A spokeshave is handy for working in close to the knees.

122 If you think sculling as a means of propulsion might be somewhere in your future, you should make provisions now. The sculling notch is centered, its size picked up from the drawings and penciled on the transom. The narrow blade of a sabersaw makes quick work of this operation. The corners of the transom and the notch can now be well rounded and sanded smooth.

123 A round wood rasp, used to put a "scallop" on the ends of the rail spacer blocks, creates a detail well worth the time. In any event, the rail tops need to be planed and sanded smooth, then all sharp edges given a small radius. The breasthook and quarter knees must also be smoothed into a nice transition with the rails.

124 Setting the maststep is next. To ensure a proper rake to the mast, the boat should be as level fore-and-aft as possible. Make a maststep block of mahogany and mark a centerline on it which should be aligned with the centerline on the bottom panel. Since the mast hole is already through the seat, you can use tape to plot the hole's center. Plumb down with a spirit level as shown at a random distance from the after edge of the seat, then take the measurement from the edge of the level to the hole's center.

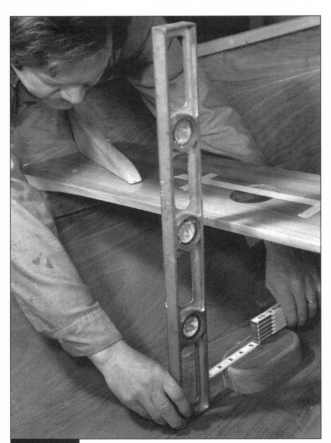

125 Now, without moving the level, position the maststep so its center is the same distance from the level's edge. Make a mark on the bottom panel at the after end of the maststep block to record this positioning, then move the block forward ½", which will rake the mast aft the proper amount.

Trace around the step, remove it, then drill pilot holes downward through the bottom panel, followed by permanent screw holes back up through.

126 The hole in which the foot of the mast will sit should now be bored in the step. I followed with a rotary rasp, which gave this hole a shape to fit the mast taper, but this shape can be worked in with a hand rasp or another tool of your choice. After cutting a small notch on the underside of the maststep to allow the hole to drain, the step can be epoxied and screwed in place.

The Outer Keel

127 The Shellback's last structural member is the outer keel. Center points have been located at either end of the bottom panel, and now a plywood straightedge is being used to connect these points with a penciled centerline. Lines parallel to this and spaced either side will be drawn to give guidelines for the edges of the outer keel.

128 My plywood keel pattern is shown here after being fitted to the hull and made with widths taken from the drawings. Its outline will now be traced onto the mahogany stock and sawn out. Notice that the forward end (farthest from view) is not cut to the curvature of the hull, but allowed to run straight, since it is narrow enough to be sprung into place.

129 The keel's edges are smoothed to a fair curve using a block plane.

130 Most of the keel's screw fastenings will be driven from inside out, so you should drill pilot holes along the centerline at about 6″ intervals to locate where these screw holes will be.

31

131 It's nice to have a helper at this point so that holes can be drilled into the keel from inside the hull while the keel is being held in position.

132 In the areas of the daggerboard case and stem it will be necessary to fasten the keel from the outside. This forwardmost hole must be counterbored deeply to allow for shaping of the forward end of the keel.

133 For added strength in the after end, the keel is bored for a ¼" machine screw. A shorter bit than what's shown here will do, but it's easier to sight along this longer one to be sure the hole follows its intended path. Prior to this, you should counterbore for the head of the machine screw. Its washer and nut will be against the inside face of the bottom panel.

134 With all the drilling dust cleared away and a bead of adhesive compound applied, bother that helper again to get the keel screwed in place. The neatest way to clean up squeezed-out compound is with the point of a pocket knife.

135 The keel's forward end must now be planed to fair into the stem face.

The Rudder, Tiller, and Oarlock Pads

136 With woodwork on the hull complete, we can now turn to the rudder assembly. Cut out a blade following the layout shown on the drawings. Edges of the underwater portion are tapered, and guidelines for this taper should be penciled in as shown here.

137 Pare through the plies with a spokeshave, watching that the glue lines remain somewhat concentric with the edge of the rudder blade. Taper to approximately a $\frac{1}{8}$" edge thickness.

138 The rudder cheeks can be made from scrap planking stock. Once they're shaped to fit, their edges should be beveled—a small but attractive detail.

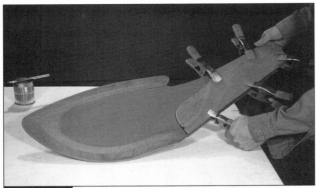

139 Spread the cheeks with epoxy, align them carefully, and clamp one on either side of the blade. Note the pattern of the finished blade taper.

140 Before any painting is done, rudder hangers should be centered on the transom at the height given on the drawings, bored for machine screws, and temporarily fastened in place.

141 The gudgeons, or rudder portion of the hangers, should be positioned to match

the transom fittings. Try the assembly before fastening to make sure it turns easily.

142 The Shellback's tiller, of ⅞" mahogany, can be cut to shape on the bandsaw. The cross-sectional shape is rectangular at the after end but gradually works to eight-sided through the midsection and then oval at the grip.

143 Tiller cheeks, also of ¼" plank scrap, should be shaped about as shown, their edges beveled slightly, and epoxied to the tiller. After the epoxy cures, hold the tiller in position and trace the outline of the cheeks onto the rudder.

144 With the rudder and tiller clamped together in their relative positions, bore a ¼" hole through all so that its center is about ½" from the after edge of the rudder.

145 Now, with the tiller set aside, run a ⅜" bit through the rudder hole. Connect the rudder edge with the hole with a couple of saw cuts to form a ⅜" or slightly wider notch.

146 With a length of ⅛" brass pipe (outside diameter ⅜") as a bushing, insert a ¼" round-head machine screw, with washers, through the tiller cheeks as shown. Secure with a hex nut. With any luck, the tiller can be swung up and over for easy removal.

147 The gudgeons can be removed while you paint the rudder, then repositioned and riveted through using copper nails cut slightly long and peened over.

148 For boats fitted with inwales and spacer blocks, the best oarlock arrangement is a conventional top-mounted socket in a wooden pad. These blocks have been milled to 1" thickness, rough-tapered on the bandsaw, and are being smoothed here to a slightly concave finished taper.

149 Although the amount of rail curve in 9″ is minimal, there is enough of it to trace and cut into the pads. Their finished width should be about ⅜″ less than the width across the rails.

150 With all edges sanded smooth and the corners rounded, bore the pads to accept the oarlock sockets.

151 An option here is to let in the plate of the socket so it's flush with the pad. This involves some careful chisel work.

152 Holes are drilled to screw the socket to the pad and the pad to the rails. Use a regular twist drill bit for the corner holes, as tapered bits tend to split the wood. Screws should be countersunk so that their heads are flush with the surface.

The Daggerboard and a Cap

Finishing Details

153 Saw out the daggerboard and taper it in a similar manner to the rudder. Set the small cheeks to align with the top of the trunk with the board in place, then spread epoxy and clamp them in place. Here, the workhorse of the shop, the sanding block, is in motion again to smooth things up before painting.

155 While mostly for appearance, this half-round rubbing strip at the bottom edge of the sheer plank can also take abrasions that would mar the planking. This rubbing strip was made with a router and radius bit. It's held in place with epoxy and short wood screws. Before painting the boat, bore a hole through each sheer plank at the bow to allow the rope painter to pass around the back of the stem. The edges of these holes must be well rounded to prevent the painter from chafing.

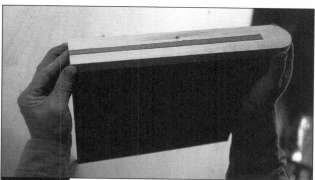

154 When the daggerboard is not in use, a cap with a tongue should be substituted to prevent water from squirting through the slot when the boat is underway or being towed. The tongue is made from the same plywood as the daggerboard and extends nearly to the bottom of the trunk. The cheeks are of cedar to match the seats, notched to accept the tongue as shown. Epoxy will hold these two pieces together. It's good to have a removable pin through the trunk sides to hold this cap in place.

156 Now that the woodworking on the hull is completed, you can start to apply coats of your favorite finish. Check once more to be sure that fastening holes, seams, and surface scratches have been filled and that everything is shaped, rounded, and sanded smooth. Your color scheme can be whatever strikes you as being appealing. Even bright colors that might be considered gaudy on larger craft can be quite attractive on a boat of this size. Here's a rundown of the finishing steps we went through on this particular boat:

One coat of white marine undercoater, thinned to brushing consistency, was applied with a 2″ natural-bristle brush and allowed to dry completely. Any surface imperfections that showed up once the hull was primed were filled with a white marine surfacing putty. The boat was then sanded with 120-grit sandpaper, which took off much of the paint but left the grain sealed. Two more coats of undercoater were brushed on, followed by two coats of marine enamel in our final color, sanding lightly with 220-grit paper between coats. Our only varnish is on the seats, daggerboard cap top, and tiller. These items were given six coats of varnish.

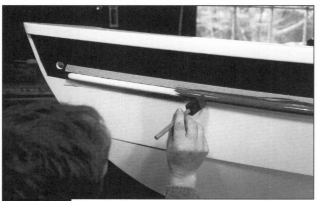

157 Painter's masking tape is helpful when you are painting one finish color up to another. A foam brush worked well for painting the half-round rubbing strip. Note the hole for the painter in the sheerstrake.

158 A ½"-wide strip of brass half-oval was attached to the bottom of the keel to provide protection when the boat is beached or dragged. The strip was first drilled and countersunk for wood screws spaced about 5" apart. That operation can be done with a drill press. Before drilling, however, the after end of the brass strip should be bent to avoid crimping at the holes. Bedding compound was spread sparingly along the edge of the keel before the strip was screwed in place.

159 If your boat will be used as a tender or where it might come in contact with other craft in an unpredictable way, some kind of gunwale guard is practically a necessity. The three-quarter round (cross-sectional shape) variety of canvas-covered rubber works well. We fastened the gunwale guard in place with ½" copper tacks (although staples could be used instead); small wood screws with washers hold up best in severe use. The upper tab is fastened first, "inside out," then the guard is folded over (hiding these fastenings) and the bottom tab is tacked along the lower edge of the wooden guardrail.

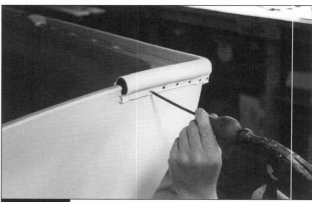

160 Because copper tacks have a reputation for bending in unbelievable ways, a small hole, started with an awl or ice pick, is used to reduce the number of casualties.

161 Rubber end trim can be purchased to finish off the gunwale guard, but pieces of leather cut to shape and tacked in place produce a somewhat more yachty appearance.

Building the Spars

162 Now we'll turn to building the mast. Our chosen material is white spruce, and since stock of sufficient thickness and quality was not readily available, we ripped up a reasonably clear 2 × 8, cutting it in half lengthwise, then stacking the two pieces to produce a nominal 4 × 4. After spreading the epoxy, we pressed most of our clamp collection into service in gluing the two pieces together.

163 To begin the mast shaping process, strike a centerline and from it lay out points representing the mast diameter at given intervals as taken from the spar plan.

164 Tack a batten through these points, sight it to a fair line, and pencil in the line. This gives the mast taper on two faces.

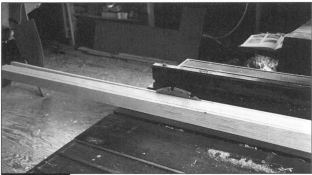

165 Much time can be saved by sawing away, rather than planing, most of the extra wood from the taper. Although we're using a tablesaw here, a bandsaw would be a more popular choice. Cut as close to the line as you can without cutting into it.

166 Use a hand plane to bring the shape down to the taper lines, making sure you keep the two surfaces square to the two original sides.

167 Lay out the taper again on one of the freshly planed sides, in the same manner as before. Cut and smooth to these lines, and you'll have a tapered, four-sided mast.

168 Now use a marking gauge to lay down the guidelines for giving the mast eight sides. Although this gauge is bored for two pencils, I'm using just one and making two passes per side.

169 Hold the mast for planing at 45° by means of a notched block clamped to one of the sawhorses; then, using the guidelines of the previous step, plane to eight sides.

170 For equal face widths, it's necessary to plane right down to the lines. Be sure you do a visual check for eight uniform sides; otherwise, the finished mast may be slightly out of round.

MAKING A MARKING GAUGE

1 So that the gauge will travel without binding, base your layout on a squared section about ½" larger than the maximum section of the spar.

2 Saw out a wooden pattern to this section, and lay out a circle that is tangent to it.

3 Using a combination square, lay off a 45° line that is tangent to the circle. Repeat this on one other adjacent corner of the pattern.

4 Select a scrap piece of softwood for your gauge and transfer points A, B, C, and D (which resulted from Steps 1–3) to it. Holes for the two pencils are centered and drilled through at points B and C, while the inner edges of the holes for small-diameter (approximately ⅜") dowels fall at points A and D.

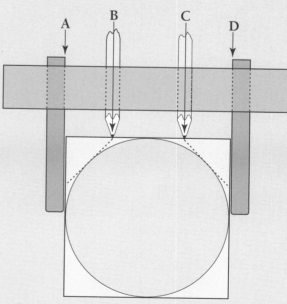

As long as the gauge is held so that both dowels are always in contact with the sides of the spar, properly proportioned lines will result.

5 Make another gauge sized for the yard and boom.

171 The eight-sided corners are planed away by eye so that you end up with 16 sides. Then, preferably using a block plane with the blade set very shallow, plane the mast round. By running your hand around the curvature you can feel little ridges that may still need your attention.

172 Finish the job with sandpaper, starting with coarse grit and working to medium/fine. The very same shaping process is followed for the

yard and boom. The spar plans for the Shellback show most ends rounded and provide the location and size of holes that need to be bored. An oil or varnish finish will protect your spars yet leave no doubt about the fact that you've been building with wood.

A Fine Pair of Oars

173 But why stop now, when we're having so much fun? Let's make some oars. We've chosen a design for a pair of 7-footers. Thin plywood patterns were made for both views of the oar. A reasonably straight-grained 2" × 8" × 10' ash plank will yield both oars if the looms (or shafts) run past each other with a blade at either end of the plank. Trace around the oar face pattern as shown, and, if both oars are to come from a single plank, make an initial cut to separate them.

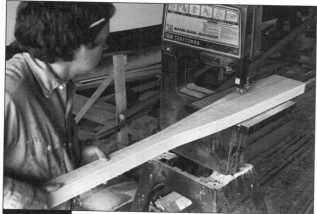

174 Saw the profile shapes of each oar...

175 ...and smooth to the line. A spokeshave works well in the concave area at the base of the blade. As with the spars, make a point of keeping the edge square to the face.

176 Tack the other (taper) pattern along each edge as shown here. If the blank has any slight warping, you can correct this by sighting this pattern straight.

177 Back to the bandsaw to cut in much of the taper. If you have a portable power plane, smoothing these surfaces—particularly when working on ash—will be considerably easier.

178 This oar's blade shape calls for a straight bevel from the profile centerline to $1/8''$ from the marked taper centerline, producing a somewhat diamond-shaped cross section. This yields a blade that is very strong yet reasonably lightweight.

179 Here's one of those eight-siding gauges back in use again—probably the one from our yard and boom. Run lines the length of the loom.

180 By now it's obvious that sparmaking and oarmaking are similar crafts. The eight sides are planed in as shown. These flats will die out as they reach the oar blade.

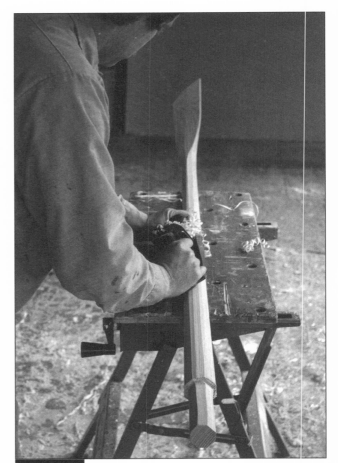

181 On to 16 sides, then to round. Give some consideration to the transition between the loom and the blade; careful shaping here should be consistent from side to side and from one oar to its partner.

182 The oar's hand grip is also given the 8–16–round treatment. For strength as well as comfort, a radius is worked in (a round rasp is being used here) at the transition from hand grip to loom. After all shaping is completed, the oars should be thoroughly sanded and given several coats of your chosen finish.

Rigging and Sailing the Shellback Dinghy

Rigging and Sailing the Shellback Dinghy

by Joel White

RIGGING

The Shellback is designed to be a simple yet useful boat—simple to build, simple to rig, and easy and fun to sail. Once the spars are made and varnished (or painted), the maststep is in place, and the sail is on hand, you are ready to rig the boat. This should only take an hour or two, once the materials are assembled.

You will need about 50' of ¼" Dacron rope. I much prefer three-strand yacht rope for its appearance and feel on the hands, but braid can be used if desired. In addition, you should have 30' of ⅛" nylon or Dacron braided line for attaching the sail to the spars, two small single blocks suitable for the ¼" mainsheet, and one small snaphook for attaching the end of the sheet to the rope traveler.

Also on hand should be three small stainless or bronze eye straps. Two of these will be used to attach the sheet blocks to the boom, the other will attach the downhaul line to the mast. Locating the latter on the mast should wait until the sail is bent on the spars and hoisted with the halyard, when its position can be determined by the sail.

Finally, you will need a way of belaying the halyard to the forward seat when the sail is hoisted. I prefer a small hardwood belaying pin inserted in a hole in the forward seat (shown on the plans) which can be easily removed when rowing the boat.

For tools, you'll need a sharp knife, a small drill and screwdriver, a needle and waxed thread for whipping the ends of the halyard and mainsheet, and a hot knife or other device for burning the ends of the synthetic rope and line. A small propane-type burner will serve well if a hot knife is not available.

Start by seizing the upper corners of the sail to the ends of the yard, the forward end first, using the braided ⅛" line (Photo 1). Then stretch the peak out snugly to the end of the yard, and attach with a second seizing of ⅛" line (Photo 2). Each seizing should consist of at least two turns between the grommet and the hole in

the spar, and one or two turns through the grommet and around the spar itself, to prevent the sail from pulling away from the spar when under strain. After the sail is stretched along the yard, lace it to the spar with more of the ⅛" line, starting with a bowline through the corner grommet, then spiral or half-hitch turns through the grommets along the head of the sail, and finish by tying off to the other corner grommet. This lacing need be just tight enough to keep the sail close to the yard (Photo 3). Using the hot knife or applying a torch to the ends of the light line will prevent fraying.

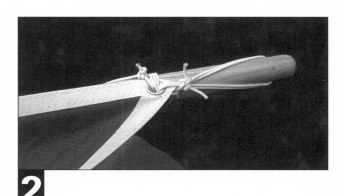

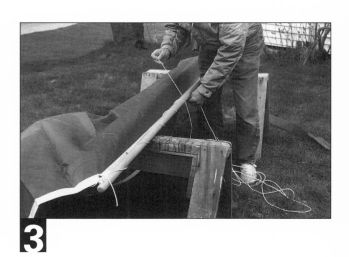

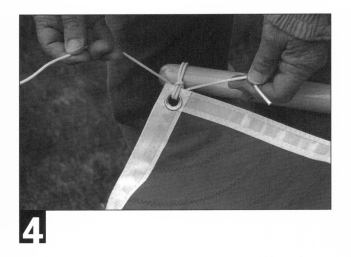

4

I like to be able to quickly adjust the clew outhaul, and to help this, I recently found a small brass ring at the local chandlery, about 1½" in diameter. I now have my clew grommet attached to this ring with a seizing. The ring is slid over the end of the boom, and the sail adjusted in or out with a piece of ⅛" line attached to the end of the boom, passed through the clew grommet, back out through the hole in the end of the boom, and then forward under the boom to a small cleat 3–4' forward of the after end. I can now adjust the outhaul while sailing if I like.

Next, lay the boom along the foot of the sail, and attach the tack (the forward corner) to the boom with a lashing similar to the one at the forward end of the yard. Be sure to leave enough space in the tack grommet to pass a length of the ¼" Dacron line through for a downhaul (Photo 4). The clew of the sail (after end) then needs to be attached to the boom with an outhaul seizing. The sail will set best and drive the boat most efficiently if the foot of the sail has some slack in it, so that it can take a nicely curved shape. If the sail is attached to the boom at each end and allowed to hang in its natural curve, there should be about 6-10" of space between the boom and the sail. Using ⅛" line, tie a bowline through the clew grommet, and pass a turn through the hole in the end of the boom to keep the sail close. Tie it off, but leave a couple of feet of extra line so that adjustments can be made in the future (Photo 5).

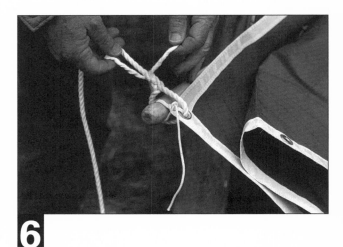

6

Finally, pass a length of ¼" Dacron line through the tack grommet and turn in an eyesplice as shown in Photo 6. The other end of this downhaul line should then be whipped and burned to a length of about 30". The sail is now properly attached to the spars.

The mainsheet blocks must be attached to the underside of the boom, using the eye straps and a couple of ¾" round-head screws each. One block should be placed 20" forward of the after end of the boom, the other about 6' forward of the after end (Photos 7–8).

5

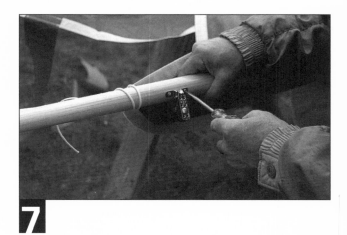

7

8

10

If you have not already bored traveler holes through the quarter knees, do so now. A 4½' piece of the ¼" Dacron is then passed through these holes and figure-eight knots tied in the ends under the knees. The traveler should be just long enough to be able to drop over the after edge of the rudder when the rudder is mounted on the stern; this allows the tiller to be easily attached to the rudderhead (Photo 9).

Cut a 20' length of your ¼" line, eyesplice one end to the snaphook (Photo 10) and whip and burn the

9

other end, then reeve off through the mainsheet blocks, with the snaphook aft.

Cut a 22' length of ¼" line for the halyard and whip and burn both ends. Tie one end to the yard about 42" from the forward end, using a clove hitch and half hitch (Photo 11). Reeve the other end through the halyard slot in the top of the mast. Place the belaying pin in its hole in the forward seat.

You are now ready to fit the rig to the boat. With the boat on your lawn, or on a float, step the mast, hoist the sail all the way up, and belay the halyard to the pin. (It helps to do this on a calm day the first time, as the next steps are easier if sail and spars are not whipping about over your head.) When the sail is fully hoisted, grasp the downhaul line and pull the tack of the sail snugly down toward the base of the mast (Photo 12). With a pencil, mark the after side of the mast about

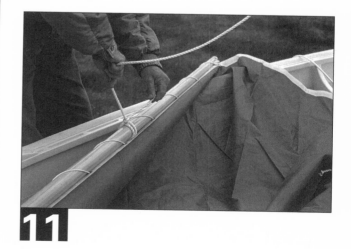

11

1' below the boom, being sure you have strong pressure downward on the tack. You can then attach your remaining eye strap to the mast at this location (Photo 13). The downhaul is then passed through this eye strap and snugged down tightly (Photo 14).

All that remains is to snap the mainsheet to the traveler (Photo 15) and tie a figure-eight knot at its forward end to ensure that it will not unreeve through the blocks.

SAILING

Now you're ready for the fun! Pick a day with gentle to moderate breezes for your first sail—a chance to get to know your new boat a bit before putting her to the test of harder winds.

Put the boat in the water, ship the rudder and tiller, and drop the daggerboard into its trunk. There should be a small hole drilled through the upper part of the daggerboard trunk and daggerboard (shown on the plans) and a $\frac{1}{8}$" x 1$\frac{1}{2}$" brass cotter pin inserted through, to keep the daggerboard in the down position. It also serves to hold the trunk cap in position when the daggerboard is stowed.

Be sure the mainsheet is free to run, hoist the sail, and coil the halyard. You are ready to go!

Shove off from the dock or mooring, fill away on to one tack or the other, trim your sheet, and check the set of your sail. It should present a clean, smoothly curved surface to the wind. If it does not, it may need adjustments to the clew outhaul, the halyard, or downhaul. Sometimes moving the attachment point of the halyard up or down the yard will improve the set. I like to have my sail with the boom steeved nicely upward, as it gives more headroom when coming about, and it looks better.

The Shellback is a light boat, and she moves easily in light airs. For the same reason, she does not have great momentum and accordingly needs to be sailed at all times. She will not carry her way far without the horsepower, or driving force, from the full sail. Also, because she is a light boat, she is very sensitive to how she is trimmed—trim of the boat in the water, and trim of the sails. She does not like to be pinched too tightly into the wind, and will quickly slow down or stop when this happens.

Sailing the Shellback to windward requires concentration. The least bit of overtrimming or pinching, and you will feel the boat slow down. In general, the boom should not be trimmed in so far that it is over the corner of the stern. By watching the luff of the sail carefully, you will soon develop the knack of keeping the sail full and drawing, and compensating for slight wind shifts. Because of her sensitivity, the Shellback is a good boat for teaching youngsters to sail, since inattention becomes so quickly noticeable.

Off the wind, sail the boat reasonably upright, and adjust the sail trim to the wind, keeping the sail full at all times and not luffing. Running before the wind, the sail can be let right out, as there are no stays to interfere. In fact, the sail can be let out to the point where it blows out ahead of the boat—which is sometimes a useful way to slow her down or to ease her through heavy puffs.

When tacking, smooth execution helps the boat pass through the eye of the wind without losing way, so do not try to tack too fast. A gradual increase in rudder angle will sail her through. When it is blowing hard, her light weight and lack of momentum will cause her to lose way quickly when tacking, and extra care may be needed to carry her across. Be sure to have full headway on before the tack, and sail her through in a smooth arc. The boat itself should be trimmed so that the stern is not immersed in the water, because it will slow her down significantly. With one person in the boat, sit either on the center seat or on the bottom just aft of it. With two people, one can sit forward of the daggerboard trunk, the other aft of the center seat. But by all means keep the stern from dragging water.

The Shellback is quick and responsive enough be a source of pleasure for people of all ages, for many years to come. If you can inspire friends and neighbors to build others, you may soon have a small fleet to row and sail with, and to race against. Such gatherings are inexpensive, uncomplicated, and wonderful fun.

ROWING

Rowing the Shellback is usually a great pleasure, unless you're pulling hard against high wind and steep chop. Feathering the oars in such conditions helps a bit, and rowing side-by-side with another person makes it much easier, as long as you can keep the rhythm synchronized. When rowing a passenger, it is normally best if you row from the forward position while the passenger sits aft, in order for the boat to trim properly. Otherwise, the stern settles too much, and the transom drags water.

SAILING

The Shellback is quite responsive under sail, and all it takes is a little time to become used to her ways. The main objective is to keep her sail full and driving, and not to try and pinch her to windward. By the same token, the trim of the boat itself will affect boat speed, the most important aspect of which is to prevent the transom from dragging water. Keep in mind that in higher winds and gusty conditions, any open boat is easily subject to capsizing and swamping. Use caution in these conditions, and exercise prudent seamanship. Have a row of reefpoints sewn into your sail, and reef early if the wind pipes up. If you want the Shellback to float higher in the water in the event of a capsize, you can add blocks of flotation under the seats.

SCULLING

The Shellback is easily sculled with one oar in the sculling notch, a handy arrangement for entering a crowded dinghy float, or for propelling oneself around a quiet harbor while having some liquid refreshment. Sculling is a traditional form of propulsion still used among working boats in certain areas, and it is a skill worth preserving. Some people stand, some sit, and others kneel in their boats while sculling. Do whatever is comfortable.

Shellback Study Plans

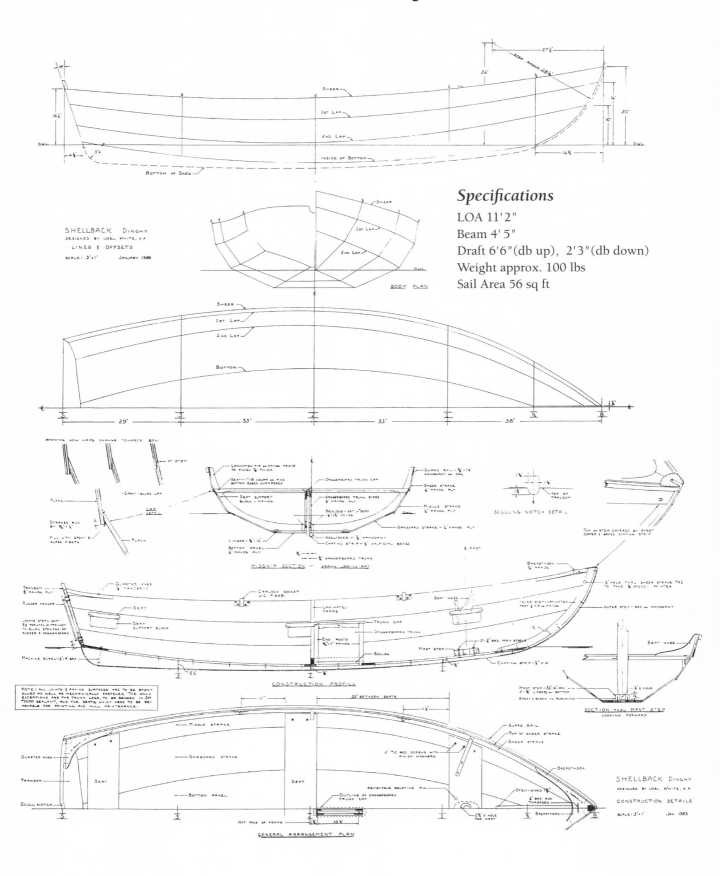

Specifications

LOA 11'2"
Beam 4' 5"
Draft 6'6"(db up), 2'3"(db down)
Weight approx. 100 lbs
Sail Area 56 sq ft

SHELLBACK DINGHY
DESIGNED BY JOEL WHITE, N.A
LINES & OFFSETS
SCALE: 3"=1'   JANUARY 1989

BODY PLAN

More Good Reading from WoodenBoat Books

Herreshoff of Bristol
A Photographic History of America's Greatest Yacht and Boat Builders
by Maynard Bray and Carlton Pinheiro

An in-depth look at the inner workings of America's greatest yacht construction yard, from 1898 to 1946. Herreshoff's built the fastest sail and steam yachts of its time and was responsible for many of the innovations that define the modern yachts of today. With more than 250 previously unpublished photographs, reproduced in luxurious duotone, this volume provides a history of the firm and the remarkable men, Nathanael and John, who founded it. Includes an appreciation of the revolutionary building methods employed by the firm and shows in detail their system of framing and planking, the casting of lead keels, and the launching of magnificent yachts built to unparalleled standards.

256 pg., illus., hardcover
#325-085 Ship Wt. 3 lbs $49.95

How to Build the Haven 12½-Footer
by Maynard Bray

Developed by Joel White for a client who loved the Herreshoff 12½, but required a shallow draft, the Haven 12½ is a keel/centerboard variation of the original. This book will show you how to construct her using the same process used to build the original Herreshoffs in Bristol, Rhode Island. She's built upside down, with a mold for every frame. No lofting is required. Each step in this unique process is carefully explained and illustrated, which, with detailed construction plans, provides a thorough guide for advanced amateurs.

64 pg., illus., softcover
#325-077 Ship Wt. ½ lb $15.00

How to Build a Wooden Boat
by David C. "Bud" McIntosh
Illustrated by Samuel F. Manning

Everything you need to know to construct a cruising boat with no more than a set of plans, a pile of lumber, and determination. Written and illustrated by experienced boatbuilders, *How to Build a Wooden Boat* covers the entire process, from lofting to finishing out. Setting up molds, lining off, ribbands, steaming and fitting frames, planking, pouring the keel, bulkheads and floorboards, decks, rudders, spars, the works. Written with style, humor, and, above all else, clarity.

264 pg., over 200 illus., hardcover
#325-075 Ship Wt. 2½ lbs $36.00

The Expectant Father's Cradle Boat Book

by Peter Spectre and Buckley Smith

A wonderful and engaging book for anyone who wants to create something special for a new baby. *The Expectant Father's Cradle Boat Book* is your guide to the design and construction of traditional cradle boats for infant children. Inspired by a series of cradle boats that have been featured in numerous issues of *WoodenBoat*, this book contains instructions and patterns for two different types of cradle boats, a gallery of photographs of a variety of completed cradles, and an appendix of sources of supply. If you can handle basic woodworking tools and follow directions, you'll find building a cradle boat both simple and satisfying.

96 pg., illus., softcover
325-095 Ship Wt. ½ lb $14.95

Keeping the Cutting Edge

by Harold H. Payson

A valuable manual for all woodworkers. Written by a professional boatbuilder who abhors dull saws, this book tells you how to sharpen and maintain all types- handsaws, bow and buck saws, powersaw blades, dado sets, bandsaws, chainsaws, and more. It is packed with tips, including descriptions of a variety of jigs and special tools, and never leaves you in doubt about what to do in even the most difficult sharpening situation. This heavily illustrated shop manual contains everything you need to know to keep your cutting edges sharp.

32 pg., illus., softcover
#325-015 Ship Wt. ½ lb $7.95

The Shipcarver's Handbook

by Jay S. Hanna

A carver for over 40 years, Jay Hanna takes you through the steps of traditional marine carving in this revised and expanded version of his *Marine Carving Handbook*. Learn how to carve sternboards, billetheads, trailboards, eagles, dolphins, rope borders, and more. Learn design and lettering, set-up and carving techniques, woods, tools and sharpening, finishing, and gold leafing. A well-illustrated, beautifully designed book that will guide and inspire both the amateur and professional.

108 pg., illus., hardcover
#325-080 Ship Wt. 1 lb $17.95

Plans & Kits Available from WoodenBoat

The Shellback Dinghy Plans

Drawn by Joel White, the six sheets of plans include: lines and offsets, building jig details, plank layout, sailing rig details, full-sized patterns for molds, frame, stem, stern, knees, and breasthook. No lofting required.
#400-109 Ship Wt. 1½ lbs $75.00

The Shellback Dinghy Kit

The kit includes all parts pre-cut, made of the highest-quality materials, plus fastenings, hardware, plans, and instructions. Choose from the sailing or rowing version.
You supply the paint and epoxy. Shipped freight-collect from Maine; please allow 2–4 weeks for delivery. (Sails sold separately.)
Sailing Kit #603-001 $1,495
Rowing Kit #603-002 $1,295

The Shellback Dinghy Model Kit

Make this model as a dry run for building the full-sized boat. This is no "snap piece A to piece B" kit—instead you will learn the actual building process, but in a table-sized scale. This is our first kit at a 3" to 1' scale, making the pieces very easy to handle. The result is a thorough understanding of glued-lapstrake plywood construction, plus a finished model measuring just over 33" long, that you can actually sail. Available Summer '94.

The Nutshell Pram Scale Model Kit

Scaled from the 7'7" Nutshell Pram, also with the purpose of helping to teach you how to build the full-sized Nutshell—from our plans or kit. We provide the wood, sail, plans, and instructions. You provide the glue, paint, and effort.
#620-001 Ship Wt. 1½ lbs $39.95

Nutshell Pram Kits

Full-sized boat kits available in 7'7" or 9'6" versions. As with the Shellback, the kit includes pre-cut wood, fastenings, hardware, plans, and instructions. Shipped freight-collect from Maine. Please allow 2–4 weeks for delivery. (Sails sold separately.)
9'6" Sailing Kit #605-002 $1,150
9'6" Rowing Kit #605-001 $950
7'7" Sailing Kit #600-002 $850
7'7" Rowing Kit #600-001 $700

How to Order

PHONE ORDERS
TOLL-FREE U.S. & Canada:
1-800-225-5205
Overseas: 207-359-4647
FAX: 207-359-8920
Mon.–Fri., 8 a.m.–6 p.m. EST
Sat. 9–5, Oct.–Dec.

Please fill out the order form before you call. It is your record of the order. Use the info below to figure shipping costs. We will ask for your catalog code, which is located after your phone # on the right side of your order form.

VISA, MASTERCARD & DISCOVER ARE WELCOME

OR WRITE:
The WoodenBoat Store
P.O. Box 78
Brooklin, Maine 04616

Payment must be made in U.S. dollars payable on a U.S. bank.

CUSTOMER SERVICE
If you have any questions about a product or an order, please call customer service toll-free, 1-800-225-5205.

RETURN POLICY
We want you to be pleased with every item you receive. If you are not, just return it for a courteous replacement, refund, or credit.

OUR GUARANTEE
Our products are guaranteed to be 100% satisfactory. Return anything that proves otherwise. We will replace it or refund your money.

SHIPPING
Please select the appropriate area shipping charge according to destination & delivery method & include that charge in the corresponding box on your order form. We ship most orders in 2 working days. For our Canadian customers: we will make an extra effort to see that your order is shipped in one package.

U.S. Shipping Charges

	Zip Code up to 49999	50000+	Two Day Delivery	Next Day Delivery
Minimum	$1.75	$1.75	$5.50	$12.00
1/2 to 1 lb.	3.00	3.00	6.00	13.00
up to 2 lbs.	3.00	3.00	8.00	14.50
up to 5 lbs.	3.50	5.00	9.50	18.50
up to 10 lbs	4.50	7.00	14.50	26.00
up to 15 lbs	5.50	9.00	19.50	31.00
ADD for each additional 5 lbs.	$1.00	$2.00	$5.00	$5.00

Alaska & Hawaii Priority Add $5.00 to Two Day and Next Day Charges

Canadian Charges	Overseas–Surface	Overseas–Priority/Air
Up to 1/2 lb. $3.00	Up to 1/2 lb. $4.00	Up to 1/2 lb. $7.00
Up to 2 lbs. 5.00	Up to 2 lbs. 7.00	Up to 1 lbs. 13.00
Up to 3 lbs. 6.50	Up to 3 lbs. 9.00	Up to 2 lbs. 22.00
Up to 4 lbs. 8.00	Up to 4 lbs. 11.00	Up to 3 lbs. 28.00
		Up to 4 lbs. 34.00
ADD $1.50 for each additional lb. Priority: ADD $2.00 to Total	ADD $2.00 for each additional lb. (Allow 2-4 months for delivery)	ADD $6.00 for each additional lb.

The WoodenBoat Store
P.O. Box 78
Brooklin, ME 04616

The WoodenBoat Store
Toll-Free U.S. & Canada: 1-800-225-5205
Overseas: 207-359-4647
Hours: 8 a.m.–6 p.m. EST, Mon. thru Fri. (Sat. 9–5, Oct.–Dec.)
FAX: 207-359-8920 anytime
(Please fax completed order form including VISA, MasterCard, or Discover card information)
Or write us: The WoodenBoat Store, P.O. Box 78, Brooklin, Maine 04616

NAME _____

ADDRESS _____

CITY/STATE/ZIP _____

SHIP TO (if different than above) _____

ADDRESS _____

CITY/STATE/ZIP _____

YOUR DAY TEL# _____

Catalog Code	**WBP**

Pre-payment is required. Payment MUST be in U.S. funds payable on a U.S. bank,
VISA   MasterCard   Discover   Check, or Money Order.

CARD NUMBER															EXPIRES Month/Year
SIGNATURE OF CARDHOLDER															

QTY	PRODUCT #	SIZE	COLOR	ITEM	SHIP WT.	PRICE EACH	TOTAL

TOTAL LBS.	
SUB TOTAL	
Maine Residents Add Tax	
Regular Shipping	
Priority Shipping (from Chart at Left)	
TOTAL	

WoodenBoat's Guarantee...
Satisfaction or Your Money Back!

Free Catalogs from WoodenBoat

Send us your name or the name of anyone who might enjoy either or both of our FREE catalogs. Please check box(es).

☐ **Merchandise Catalog.** Tools for Learning—books, videos (rent or purchase), boat plans, model kits, clothing, tools, and more.

☐ **School Brochure.** General information on sailing and boatbuilding courses offered throughout the year.

NAME _____

ADDRESS _____

CITY/STATE/ZIP _____

NAME _____

ADDRESS _____

CITY/STATE/ZIP _____